Richard Lieberson's
Old-Time Fiddle Tunes for Guitar

Amsco Music Publishing Company
New York · London · Tokyo · Sydney · Cologne

Photographs

Page	Photographer
19	Doug Connor
22	Jean Hammons
25	Fred Ramsey
27	Jean Hammons
29	Doug Connor
36	Bob Pliskin
42	Doug Connor
44	Leslie Bauman
47	Doug Connor
49	Arthur Tress
60	Jean Hammons
62	Michael Kostiuk
64	Doug Connor
67	Julie Snow
74	Arthur Tress
93	Larry Lindsay
96	Jean Hammons
100	Mark Chester
103	Jack Delano · Library of Congress
105	George Mitchell
119	Sidney Lissner
122	Jean Hammons

e

© Amsco Music Publishing Company, 1974
A Division of Music Sales Corporation
All Rights Reserved

International Standard Book Number: 0-8256-2809-1
Library of Congress Catalog Card Number: 73-92392

Distributed throughout the world by Music Sales Corporation:

799 Broadway, New York 10003

78 Newman Street, London W1P 3LA
4-26-22 Jingumae, Shibuya-ku, Tokyo 150
27 Clarendon Street, Artarmon, Sydney NSW
Kölner Strasse 199, 5000 Cologne 90

Design by Ira Haskell
Cover photograph by Jane McWhorter

Table of Contents

Introduction 4

How to Read the Tablature 5

The Standard Notation 7

Some Notes on Flatpicking Fiddle Tunes 8

Crosspicking 9

Keys and Capo Arrangements 10

Scales 10

The Tunes 13

    The Girl I Left Behind Me 14

    Get Along Home Miss Cindy 16

    Old Molly Hare 19

    St. Anne's Reel 22

    Growling Old Man, Growling Old Woman 26

    Cripple Creek 28

    Sally Gooden 30

    Soldier's Joy 32

    The Wind That Shook the Barley 37

    The Arkansas Traveler 38

    Sailor's Hornpipe 40

    Cluck Old Hen 43

    Chicken Reel 45

    Liberty 46

    Bill Cheatham 50

    Mississippi Sawyer 52

    Fisher's Hornpipe 54

    Blackberry Blossom 56

    Miss McLeod's Reel 61

    Bully of the Town 64

    You Married My Daughter 68

    Red Haired Boy 70

    Ragtime Annie 72

    The Boys From Bluehill 76

    Texas Quickstep 78

    Acorn Hill Breakdown 80

    Forked Deer 82

    Black Mountain Rag 84

    Weave and Way 87

    Devil's Dream 90

    Billy in the Lowground 94

    Old Joe Clark 97

    Paddy on the Turnpike 99

    The Eighth of January 101

    Sail Away Ladies 104

    Flop-Eared Mule 106

    The Humors of Lisadel 109

    Salt River 111

    Stoney Creek 115

    Cotton Patch Rag 120

Intros and Tags 123

Playing Back-up 124

Suggested Listening 128

Bibliography 128

Introduction

The fiddle and banjo preceded the guitar in rural music making in this country. When the guitar began to be used regularly in old-time music during the early years of this century, it was primarily as a back-up and rhythm instrument. The Carter Family played an important part in turning the guitar into a melody instrument. Recordings by the Delmore Brothers and Hank Snow also featured a good deal of lead guitar work and influenced many musicians.

Although the guitar is not traditionally a lead instrument in string band music, more and more guitarists are learning their instruments well enough to solo. The popularity of fiddle tunes on the guitar today is largely due to the influence of Doc Watson.

While Doc Watson was probably not the first man to flatpick a fiddle tune on the guitar, his recordings and concert appearances over the last ten years have inspired leagues of guitar pickers to try their hand at fiddle tunes. Doc's clean, fast, and driving flatpicking has kept devoted guitarists including myself, glued to the phonograph, trying to copy a solo or steal a lick here and there.

Don Reno, Norman Blake, Clarence White, and Don Crary are among the other guitarists around who do good jobs with the old-time fiddle-tunes. Reno, best known for his five-string banjo work and his vocals with Bill Harrell and the late Red Smiley, is also a first-rate flatpicker. White, who performed dazzling flat-top guitar work with the Kentucky Colonels later went on to display a unique and equally impressive style on the electric guitar with the Byrds.*

Since the playing of fiddle tunes on the guitar is a relatively new development, the guitarist who gets into old-time tunes has less traditional technique to fall back on than the banjo player or fiddler, and is often left to his own devices. When working out a tune on your own, you'll often find that a lick that sounds good on the fiddle or banjo just doesn't cut it on the guitar.

Fiddle tunes played on the guitar do not provide the volume or pulse needed for dancing, but can make for some pretty and exciting music. For the novice, fiddle tunes are an excellent way to begin learning the fingerboard. The experienced guitarist will find these tunes welcome additions to his repertoire and solid vehicles for improvisation.

*Clarence White died in an automobile accident on July 15th, 1973.

How to Read the Tablature

The six lines of the tablature staff represent the six strings of the guitar, with the top line indicating the 1st or high E string:

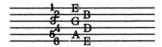

A number appearing on a line indicates where the string is to be fretted:

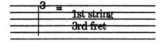

An "o" indicates the string is to be played open, or unfretted:

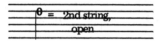

A G chord appears like this in tablature:

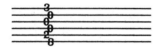

Time values are indicated as they are in standard notation:

A tie is used when the desired duration cannot be indicated with a single figure:

The note is picked *only once*.

The common figure of two eighth notes ♪ ♪ is sometimes replaced by a dotted eighth note and a sixteenth note: . Here you count  instead of . This rhythm is common in Irish tunes.

A note which is "hammered" is indicated thus:

In the above example, the 1st string, 3rd fret is fingered with the first finger of the left hand. The note is picked, and, while it is still sounding, the third finger "hammers" down on the 5th fret.

A "pull-off" is the opposite of a "hammer" and is shown like this:

Here the second note (G) is sounded by the left-hand finger pulling-off on the string.

A slide is indicated in this manner:

In this example pick the 3rd string, 2nd fret and then slide your finger up to the 4th fret.

The mark ∽ over a note indicates that you are to "bend" the note, by pushing the string upwards and against the fingerboard, raising the pitch of the note about a half-step (one fret):

Grace notes have almost no time value and are sounded very quickly, usually being hammered or sliding into other notes:

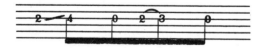

Repeat marks indicate that the piece is to be repeated from the beginning, or from the last pair of repeat marks, whichever may be the case.

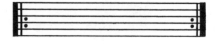

Sometimes a tune will have a separate first and second ending, indicated like this:

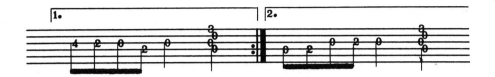

Numbers over notes in the tablature indicate the suggested left-hand fingering:

In some passages, only one or two notes are fingered; if these notes are fingered correctly, your other fingers should fall into place naturally.

The mark ➢ over a note indicates an accent.

The Standard Notation

These symbols are used in the standard notation:

A circled number appearing below a note indicates the string the note is to be played on. For instance, the following example tells you to play B on the 3rd string (4th fret) rather than the open B string. The italicized number over the note shows the suggested left-hand fingering. In many cases I have left the fingering up to the individual guitarist's discretion.

Some Notes on Flatpicking Fiddle Tunes

Before tackling any of these tunes you should first master the basics of flatpicking guitar. Learn to play solid back-up and some tunes in the Carter Family style. Listen to the runs used by bluegrass guitarists such as Lester Flatt and Jimmy Martin. *Baxter's Flatpicking Manual* (Amsco) and Happy Traum's *Flatpick Country Guitar* (Oak) are both good books for the beginning flatpicker.

Most guitarists playing in this style prefer the large, dreadnought type guitar such as the popular Martin D-28 and D-18. This type of guitar has a full tone and provides the volume and projection needed when playing with a band.

Although thin picks seem easier to work with at first, a medium or heavy pick will produce a better sound and strengthen your playing.

Some flatpickers, including Doc Watson, use about three parts arm action and one part wrist when playing. Some folks will tell you that this is the *only* correct way to play, but plenty of crackerjack guitar players, including Don Reno, play largely from the wrist.

You may find that resting your little finger on the pickguard allows you some extra control and support when playing. If you do this, allow your finger to glide over the guard when it seems natural; don't plant it on one spot and refuse to move it.

The basic rule is to use a down-stroke on the beat and an up-stroke on the off-beat. For example, in this standard bluegrass run you pick down on 1, 2, 3 and 4, and up on &:

After you've been flatpicking for a little while the correct alternation of strokes will become natural to you.

Crosspicking

The above rule is abandoned in cross-picking, a syncopated technique used to good advantage by Doc Watson and Clarence White, among others. Jesse McReynolds makes extensive use of cross-picking in his famous mandolin style.

In cross-picking, two down-strokes and one up-stroke create a 123 123 12 rhythm:

This can be modified to create other rhythms:

Reverse cross-picking can also be used:

Here's a few measures of the Carter Family's *Little Rosewood Casket* with cross-picking:

Cross-picking can be used to create bluegrass banjo rhythms or to imitate the shuffle of a fiddler. It is also effective in filling out the melody in slower songs.

Keys and Capo Arrangements

The most common keys for fiddle tunes are G, C, D and A. It is generally a good idea to be able to play a tune in the fiddler's key, thus enabling you to play with other musicians. A guitarist often picks a tune in G that fiddlers know in A. In this case, the guitar player can capo up two frets. This is also commonly done with tunes in D that guitarists pick in C. When playing guitar duets it often sounds good to have the rhythm guitar play without a capo (in A or D) and the lead play capoed on the second fret (in G or C position, respectively).

Scales

It will be useful to learn the scales of the keys you will use most often:

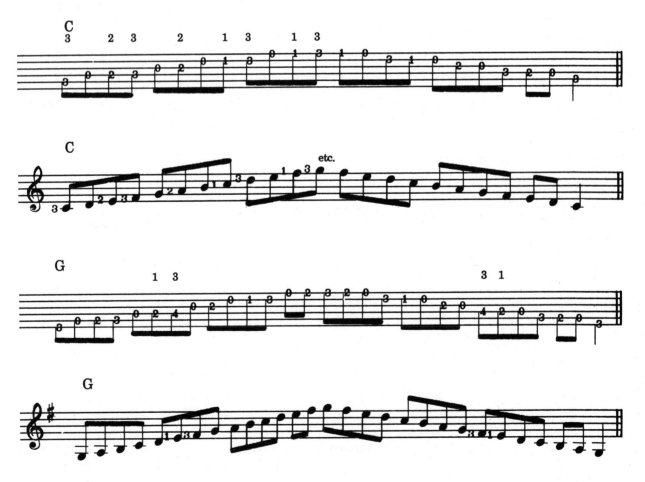

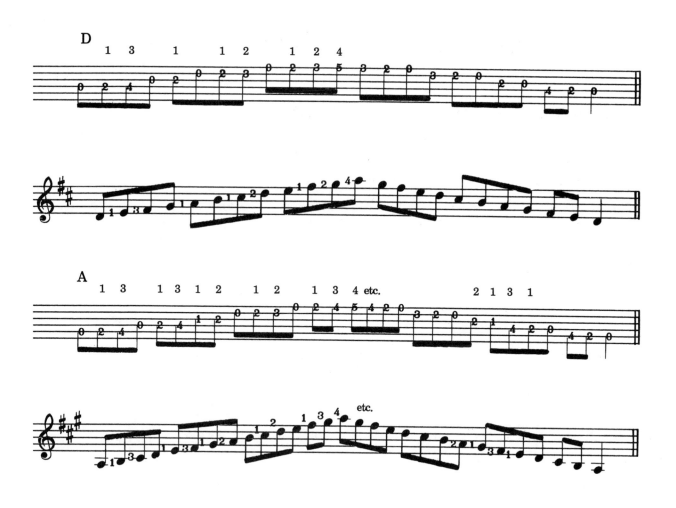

Closed position scales (those not using the open strings) can also be used. Here is the D scale in several positions:

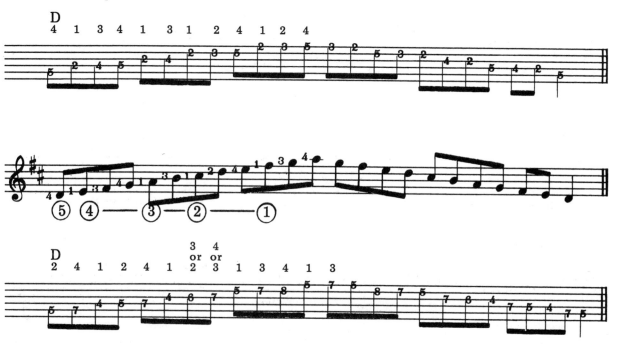

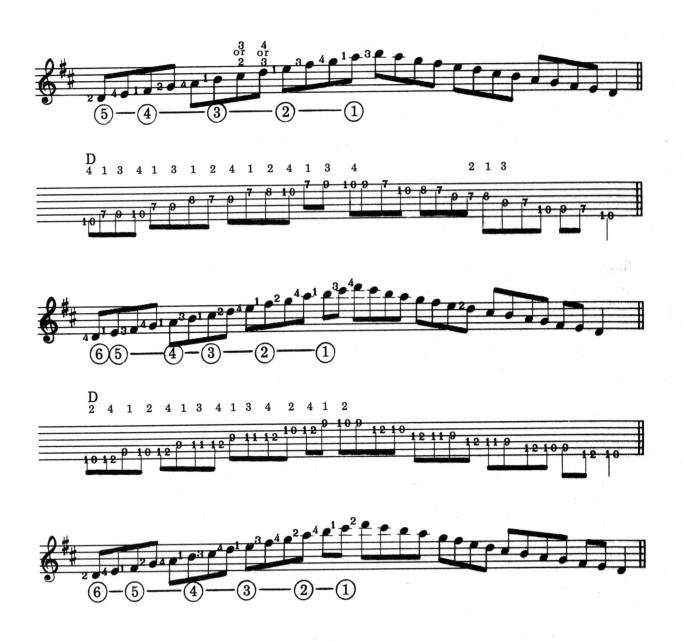

Note that these closed position scales are movable and may be used anywhere on the fingerboard.

A finger rolling technique in which two successive notes are fretted with the same finger will be helpful in playing some passages.

In the example from *Red Haired Boy* fret the E (4th string, 2nd fret) with your first finger, and then *roll* downwards on the tip of your finger until contact is made with A on the 3rd string (2nd fret). Do not flatten your finger when doing this. This rolling motion takes place in the opposite direction in the example from *Black Mountain Rag*.

A note will occasionally be preceded by a quick arpeggio:

To execute this let your pick quickly glide over the top four strings, letting only the last note (in this case A) ring out. The other notes are cut short by removing each left hand finger immediately after its respective note is sounded. At the end of the arpeggio, only the 1st string should remain fretted—this is the note that you are building up to.

The Tunes

Some of the following arrangements include variations and harmony parts (for second guitar). If you are a newcomer to flatpicking you may decide to skip the variations and harmonies, which are generally more difficult than the tunes themselves.

These arrangements should provide you with some ideas on how to embellish the basic melody of a tune and improvise on it. They contain many licks that can be altered a little and used elsewhere. Some of the variations have the feel of improvised breaks and should not necessarily be learned by rote, note for note.

Although repeat marks are used at the end of each variation, it is not necessary to repeat the exact same variation the second time through. Altering a phrase, introducing a new syncopation or taking off on an improvisation will make your solos more interesting.

The best way to develop a feel for improvising is by listening to and playing with good country musicians. Fiddlers, mandolin players and banjo pickers should be as influential in shaping your style as other guitarists.

The majority of these tunes have an AABB structure: two parts, each repeated once. For some ideas on how to kick off and end the tunes, refer to the "Intros and Tags" chapter.

One last word: it is not necessary to play all these tunes at breakneck tempos. Many of them will sound better at medium speeds. In Ireland, reels and especially hornpipes are traditionally taken at a much slower pace than they are here. A good deal of Texas fiddling is done at a medium pace, suitable for "two-step" dancing, with the rhythm guitarist playing "sock" style rhythm. The beauty of many of the Irish and French-Canadian tunes will be lost if they are taken at breakdown speeds.

The Girl I Left Behind Me

This familiar tune is very simple. I don't know if it actually was popular during the American Revolution, but a number of old films have left me associating *The Girl I Left Behind Me* with the "Spirit of '76."

15

Get Along Home Miss Cindy

Learned from various sources, including Pope's Arkansas Mountaineers (County 518).

I went up on the mountain,
I gave my horn a blow,
I thought I heard my true love say
"Yonder comes my beau."

I went up on the mountain,
I heard a rabbit sneeze,
I hollered back to Liza Jane
To put on the fire please.

I would not marry a widow,
I'll tell you the reason why,
She's got so many children,
It'll make them biscuits fly.

In the opening phrase of this piece you'll be sliding into a G position on the 3rd fret:

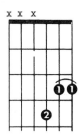

When filling out the rhythm in a measure such as this one, the number of strings you sound on the up and down strums is approximate:

Feel free to sound more (or fewer) strings than are indicated in the notation.

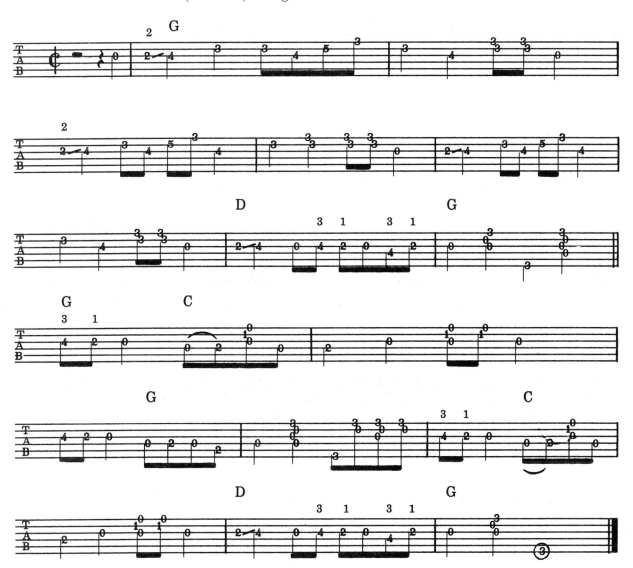

Get Along Home Cindy

Old Molly Hare

I've provided this old-timer with a harmony part for second guitar and a variation.

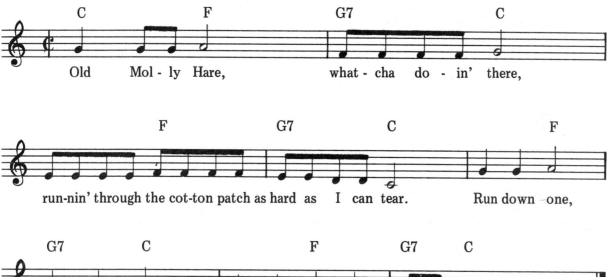

Old Mol-ly Hare, what-cha do-in' there,

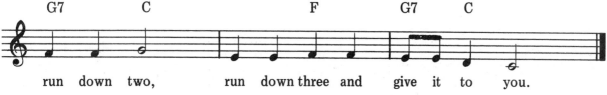

run-nin' through the cot-ton patch as hard as I can tear. Run down one,

run down two, run down three and give it to you.

Old Molly Hare, whatcha doin' there,
Running through the cotton patch as hard as I can tear.
Run down one, run down two,
Run down three and give it to you.

Step back, step back, daddy shot a bear,
Shot him through the eye and he never touched a hair.
Old Molly Hare, whatcha doin' there,
Running through the cotton patch, smoking a cigar.

Old Molly Hare

Harmony

Variation

St. Anne's Reel

Here's a real pretty one that's long been one of my favorites. The rhythm guitarist can play a Dm chord in place of the F in the B section. See which sound suits you the best. The Riendeau Family does a particularly fine rendition of this tune on their album (County 725).

When playing this measure finger an F triad on the inside strings and then slide it up for the G part.

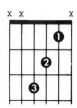

In the opening of the A part variation hold down this position:

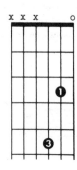

22

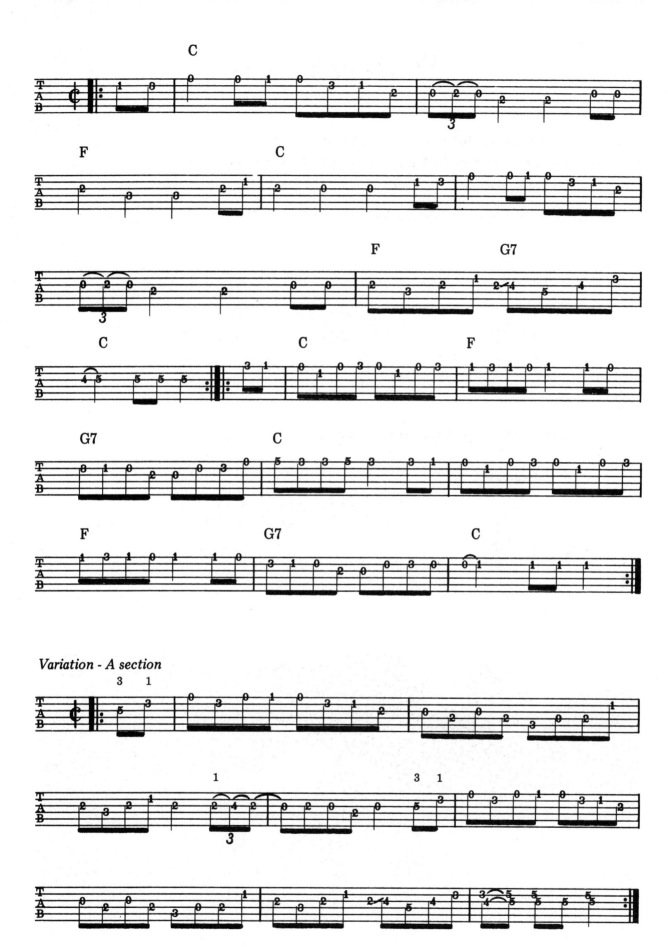

Variation - A section

St. Anne's Reel

Variation - A section

Growling Old Man, Growling Old Woman

This tune is said to portray an argument between a man and his wife, the high part representing the woman and the low part her husband. Both the major and minor third and the flatted seventh of the A scale appear in the melody. The Riendeau Family from New England gives a striking performance of this on their album. The Riendeaus do some beautiful fiddling in the French-Canadian style and play a number of tunes not often heard (some of which work out nicely on the guitar).

In the B section, a partial A chord will be used.

This position will appear in many of the tunes in A.

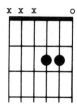

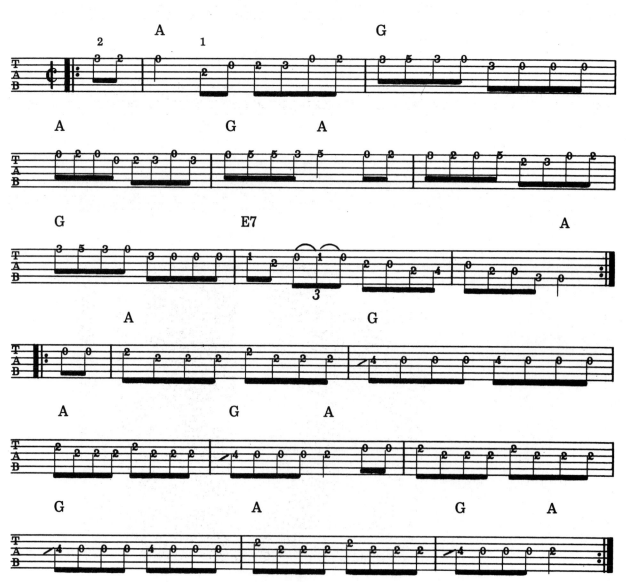

Cripple Creek

Hold your G position through the first measure.

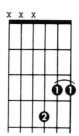

Keep the position in the second bar and hammer down your third and fourth fingers, creating a C position:

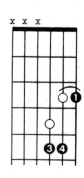

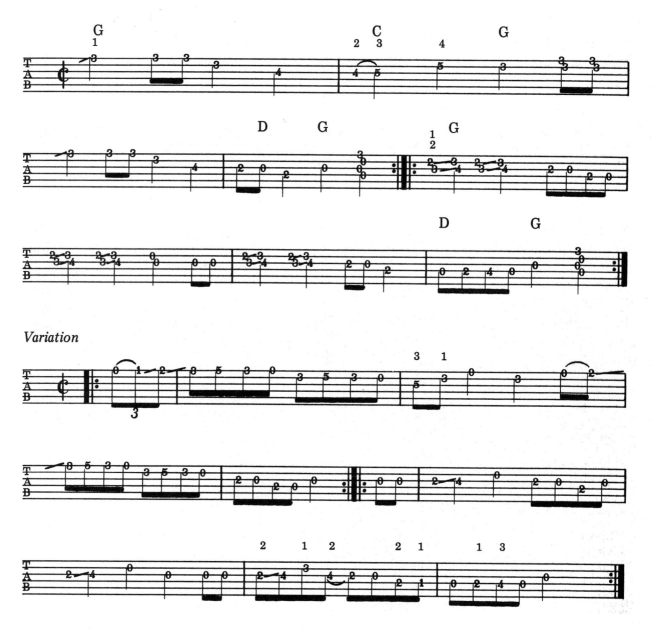

Variation

28

Variation

Sally Gooden

Don Reno and Clarence White both flatpick good versions of this standard. The fingering here may seem a bit tricky at first.

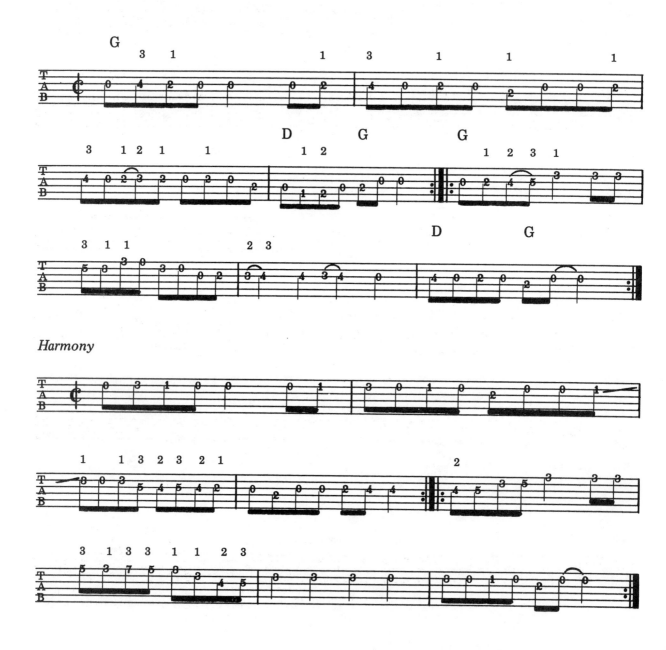

Harmony

Had a piece of pie, had a piece of pudd-in', Give it all a-way for to see Sal-ly Good-en.

Soldier's Joy

Soldier's Joy is popular on all the string band instruments. The lyrics printed here are some of those sung by Riley Puckett on his recording of the tune with Gid Tanner and the Skillet Lickers.

If you review your D scale the fingering for this tune should be easy. The phrase

in the harmony may be easier if you keep this position down:

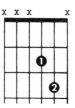

Running over the VII pos. D scale given in the "Notes on Flatpicking" chapter will aid your fingering in the harmony part.

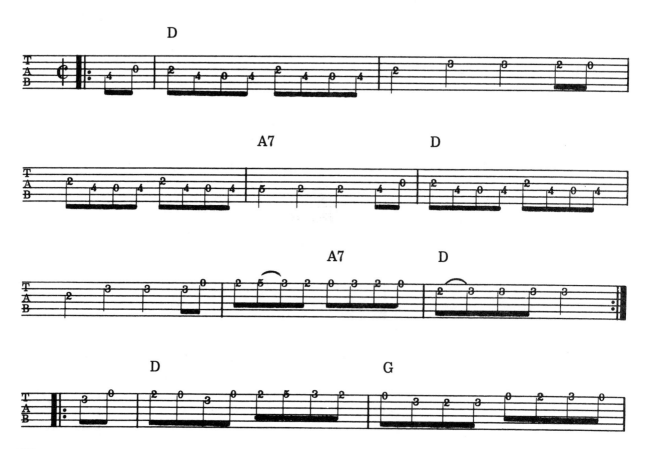

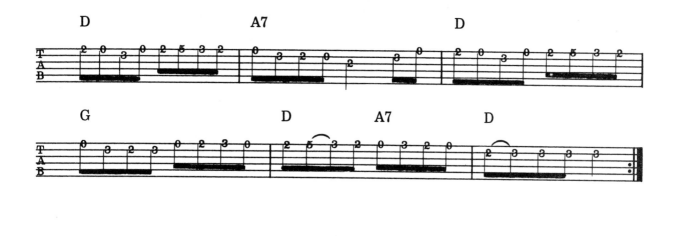

Harmony

Soldier's Joy

I am my mother's darling boy, I
am my mo-ther's dar-ling boy, I am my mo-ther's
dar-ling boy, sing a lit-tle song called Sol-dier's Joy

I am my mother's darling boy (3x)
Sing a little song called Soldier's Joy.

Grasshopper sitting on a sweet potato vine (3x)
Along come a chicken and says "it's mine."

I'm gonna get a drink, don't you want to go, (3x)
Hold on Soldier's Joy.

Twenty five cents for the morphine,
Fifteen cents for the beer,
Twenty five cents for the morphine,
Gonna drink me away from here.

The Wind That Shook The Barley

The Arkansas Traveler

The Arkansas Traveler is often accompanied by a long string of farmer-stranger jokes. David Bromberg and Norman Blake flatpick a fine twin guitar version on *David Bromberg* (Columbia C 31104).

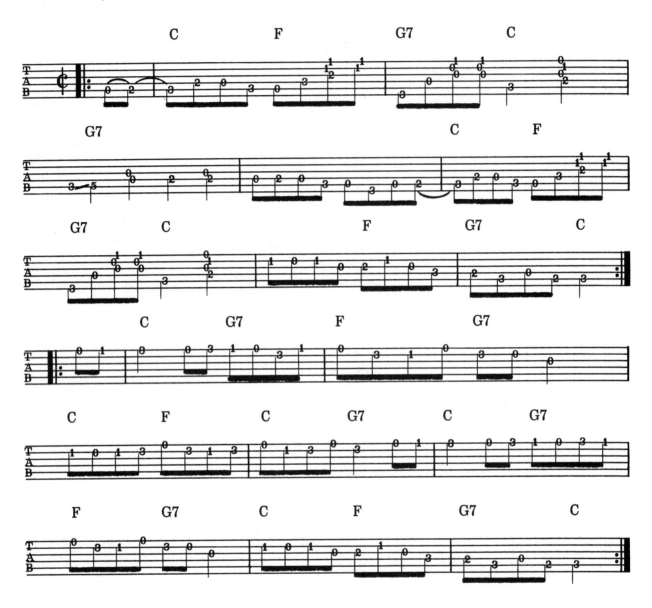

Sailor's Hornpipe

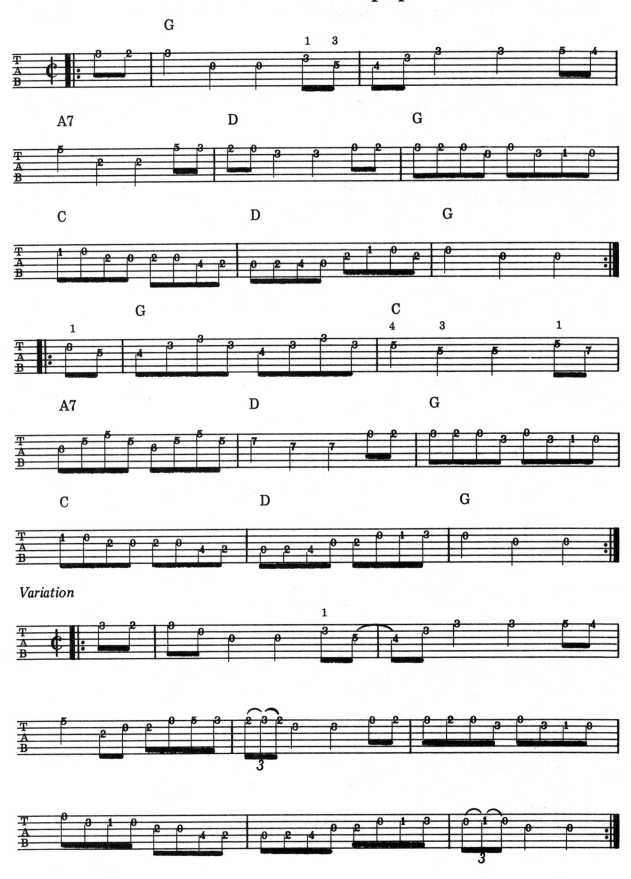

Variation

Cluck Old Hen

Kyle Creed and Fred Cockerham do a great banjo-fiddle duet of this tune on *Clawhammer Banjo* (County 701).

When playing the phrase,

pick the open E string (1st) as your finger slides into E on the 2nd string (5th fret), so that the two notes sound together.

Chicken Reel

Although this is fiddled in D, I have worked it out in E; if you're playing with a string band, it won't be too much trouble to arrange it in the original key.

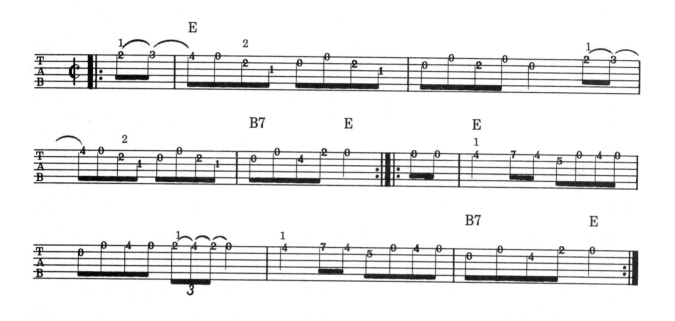

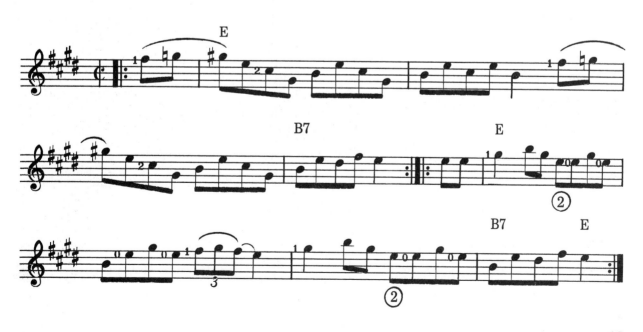

Liberty

Notice how in the first ending the note E is anticipated, falling on the second eighth rather than on the second beat of the bar.

Here is how the measure would appear without the anticipation:

This is a rhythmic device often used in fiddle tunes.

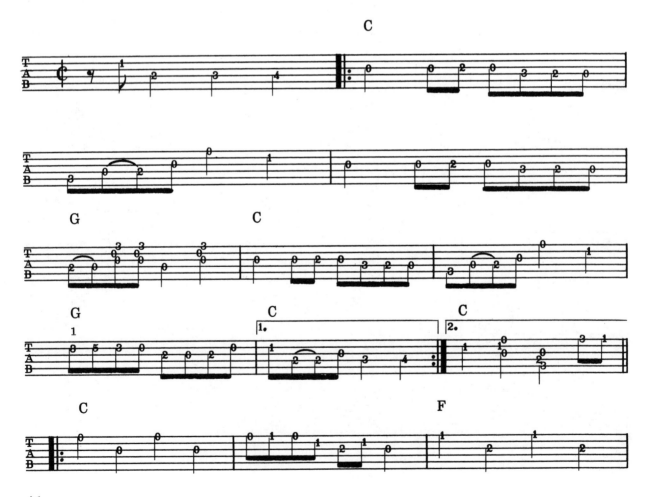

Variation - B section

Liberty

Variation - B section

Bill Cheatham

Doc Watson picks a mean *Bill Cheatham* as part of a medley on *Doc Watson on Stage* (Vanguard VSD 9/10). Arthur Smith's great version can be heard on *Old Time Fiddle Classics* (County 507).

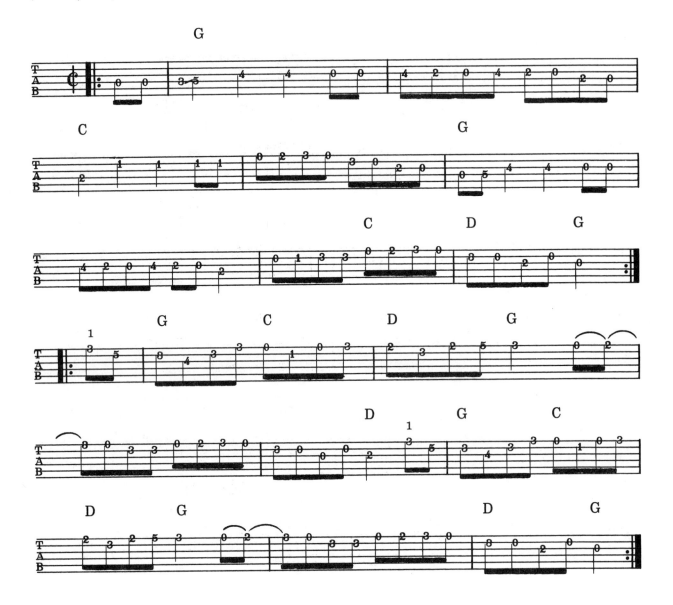

Mississippi Sawyer

*Alternate phrase:

Fisher's Hornpipe

I have heard both Irish and Texas fiddlers do beautiful things with this tune. You might try having your rhythm guitarist play "sock" style. A "sock" rhythm part for this tune is given in the "Playing Back-up" chapter.

Check out Major Franklin's version on *Texas Fiddle Favorites* (County 707).

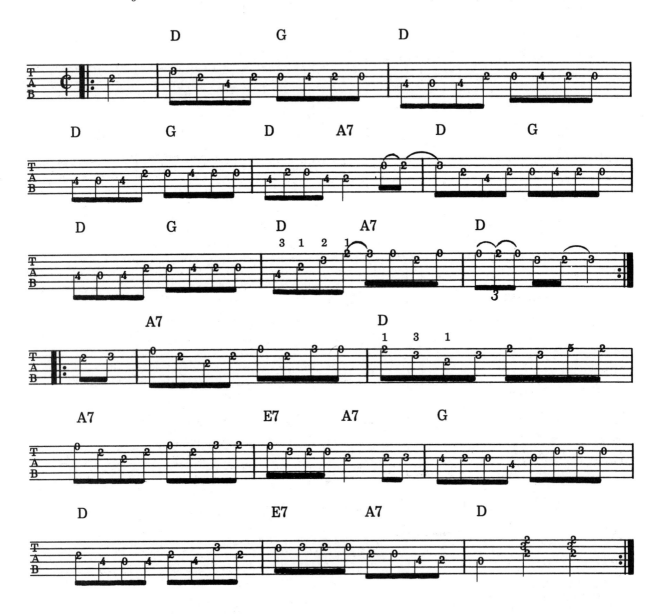

Blackberry Blossom

A fiddler camping next to me at one of the bluegrass festivals a few years ago taught me this tune. There's another tune by the same name in *Cole's One Thousand Fiddle Tunes*. Dan Crary flatpicks a hot *Blackberry Blossom* on *Bluegrass Guitar* (American Heritage AHLP 275).

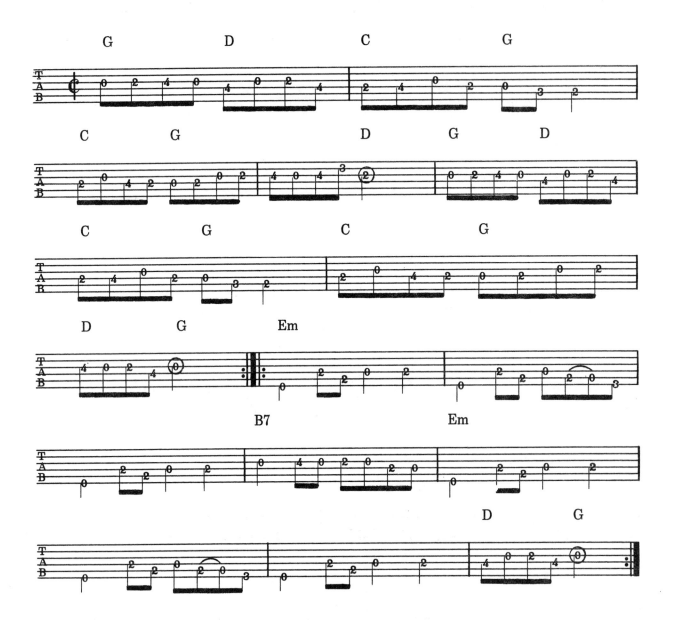

Harmony

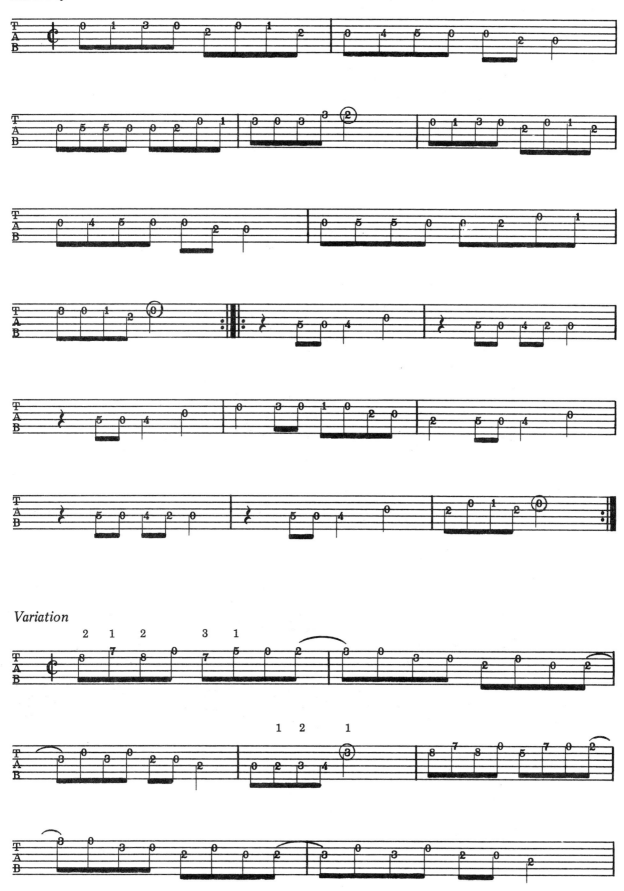

Variation

57

Blackberry Blossom

58

Harmony

Variation

Blackberry Blossom

Miss McLeod's Reel

Miss McLeod's Reel is also known in an Americanized version as *Hop High Ladies.* One well-known version was recorded by Uncle Dave Macon.

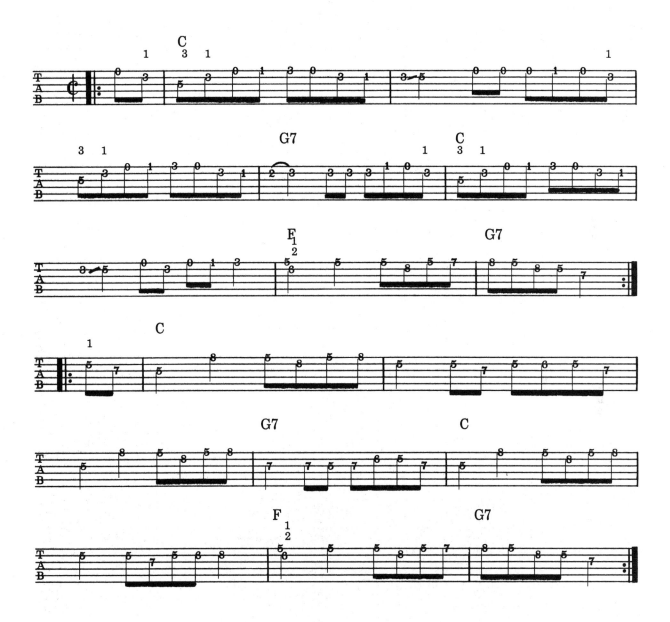

C

Have you ev-er been to meet-in' Un-cle Joe, Un-cle Joe, have you

G7   C

ev-er been to meet-in' Un-cle Joe, Un-cle Joe, have you ev-er been to meet-in' Un-cle

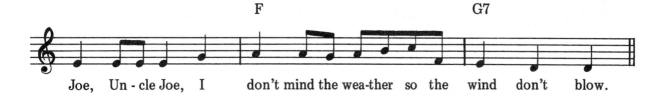

F   G7

Joe, Un-cle Joe, I don't mind the wea-ther so the wind don't blow.

Chorus:

C

Hop high la-dies for the cake's all dough,

G7   C

Hop high la-dies for the cake's all dough, Hop high la-dies for the

F   G7

cake's all dough, I don't mind the wea-ther so the wind don't blow.

Have you ever been to meetin' Uncle Joe, Uncle Joe? (3x)
I don't mind the weather so the wind don't blow.

Chorus:
Hop high ladies, the cake's all dough, (3x)
I don't mind the weather so the wind don't blow.

Does your horse carry double, Uncle Joe, Uncle Joe? (3x)
I don't mind the weather so the wind don't blow.

Chorus
How do you like the ladies, Uncle Joe, Uncle Joe? (3x)
I don't mind the weather so the wind don't blow.
Chorus

Bully of the Town

Originally an old ragtime song, *Bully of the Town* has been given a number of old-time and bluegrass treatments. The tune as played by ragtimers has a more sophisticated melody and chord progression than the version usually played by country pickers. There have been some nice finger-style versions as well as flatpicked renditions.

This tune is arranged in Carter Family style, with the melody mainly in the bass strings. You'll be holding down full chord positions more often here than in most fiddle tunes where there's a lot of single string work.

Use your "long A" position when A is called for:

This A leaves your second and third fingers free.

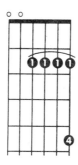

The C diminished is played like this:

Bully of the Town

You Married My Daughter
(And Yet You Didn't)

I'm sure there's a story connected with this provocatively titled tune, but I've yet to hear it. Learned from a recording by the Riendeau Family (County 725) of New England.

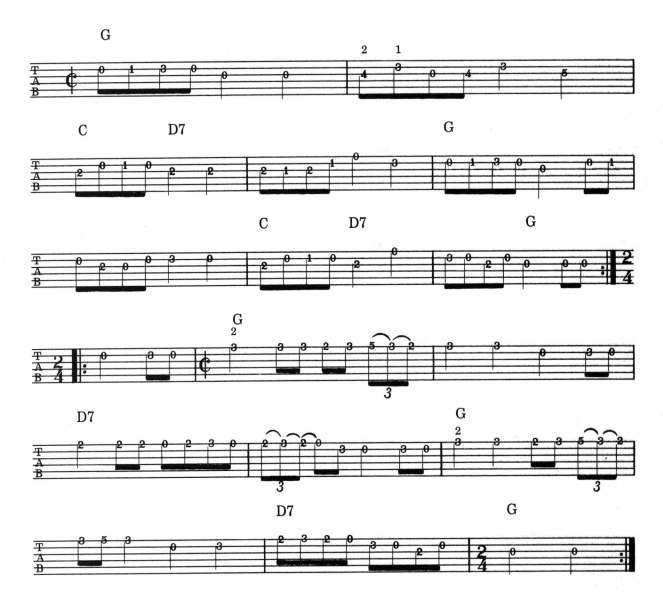

Red Haired Boy

Sometimes called *The Little Beggerman,* this old Irish tune appeared in *O'Neill's Music of Ireland.* I've heard this tune sung, although I can't recall any of the lyrics.

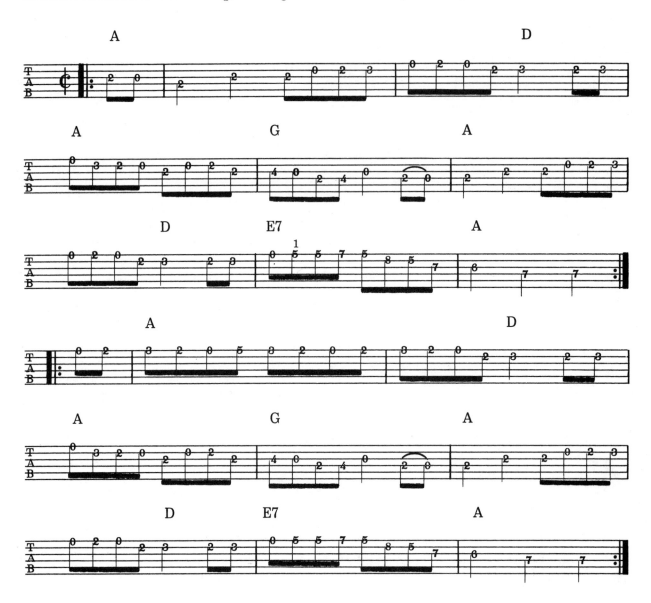

Ragtime Annie

Throughout the first three measures it will be convenient to hold a partial C chord:

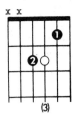

Use your third finger for the note A on the 3rd string when needed.

Doc Watson picks this as part of a medley on *Doc Watson and Son* (Vanguard VSD 79170).

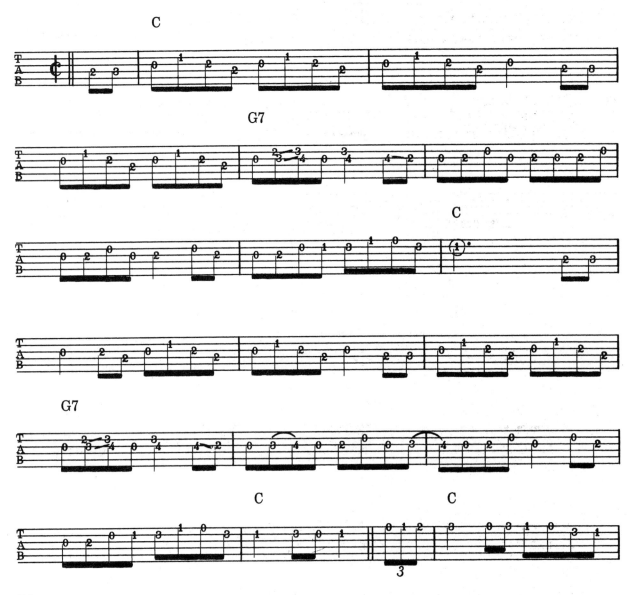

*Alternate ending

73

Ragtime Annie

The Boys From Bluehill

Here's a good Irish number learned from a guitar student of mine who picked it up from fiddler Bill Garbus.

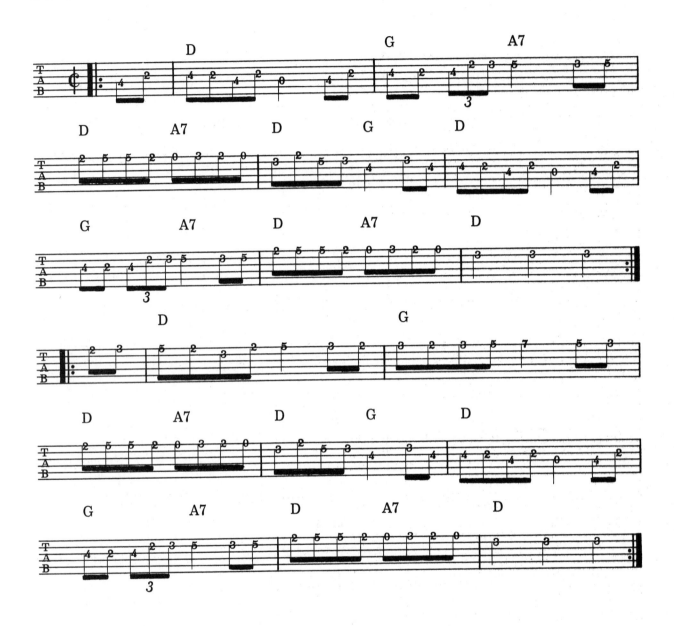

Texas Quickstep

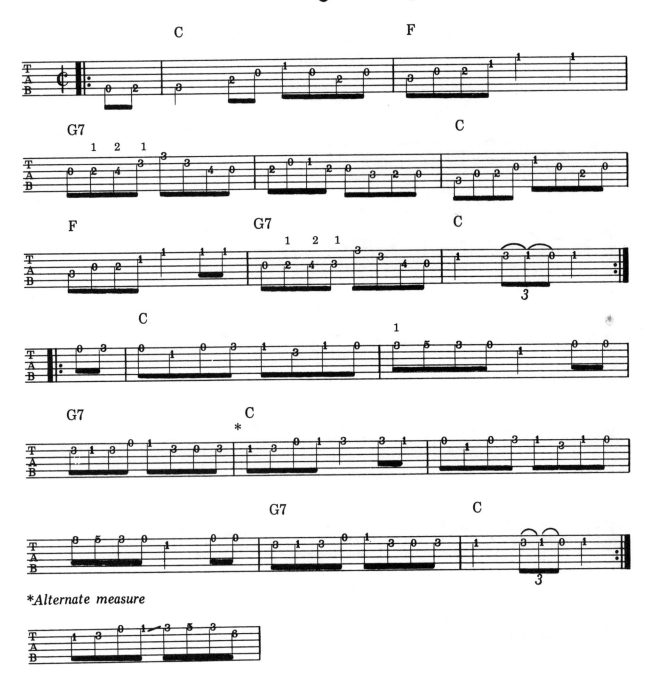

Alternate measure

Alternate measure

Acorn Hill Breakdown

Learned from Oregon fiddler Harold Allen's recording on *Fiddlin' Around* (American Heritage)

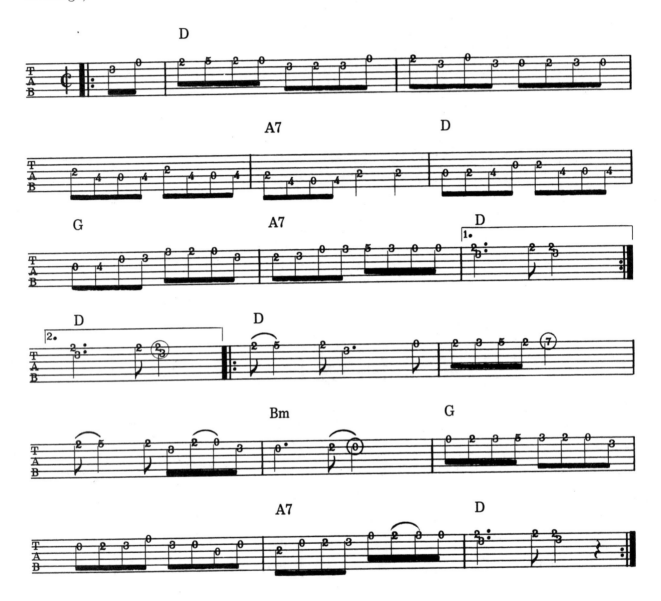

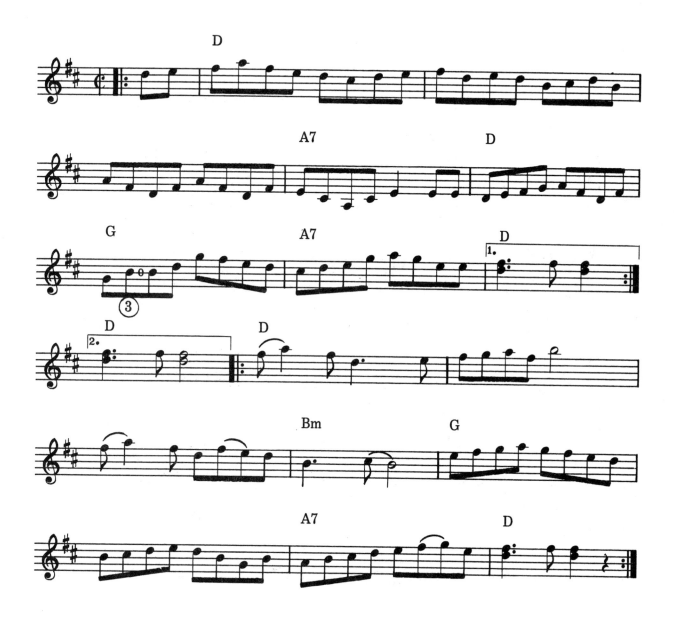

Forked Deer

Charlie Bowman & His Brothers' recording of this tune (County 527) can't be beat. Bowman's fiddling is complimented by fine back-up guitar work by Frank Wilson. I've changed the chords in the B part some, and I've stolen the last lick in the A part from Dan Crary's version.

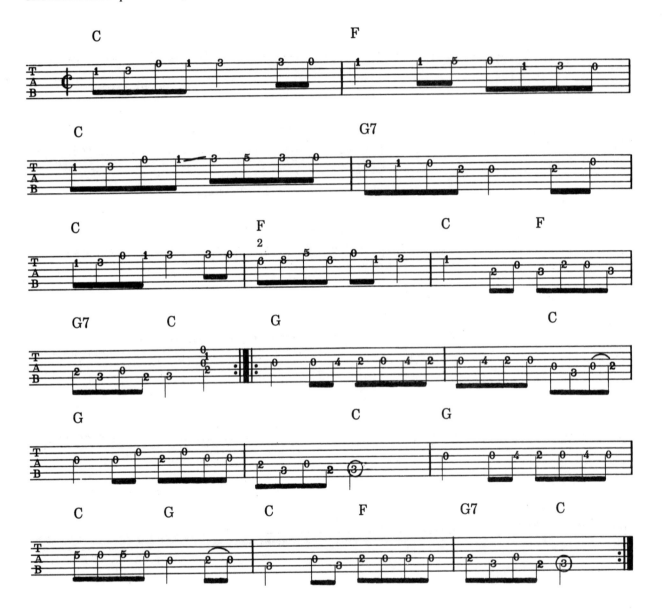

Black Mountain Rag

Doc Watson's version of this tune inspired countless numbers of guitar players to try their hand at flatpicking fiddle tunes. The tune was first done, I believe, by Leslie Keith, who fiddled with the Stanley Brothers when they were starting out. Doc picks it in C position; I've arranged it in G. Fiddlers do it in A, so just slip the old capo on the second fret and you'll be set.

Try to hear fiddler Kenny Baker's stunning *Black Mountain Rag* on *Baker's Dozen* (County 730). Kenny, who currently fiddles with Bill Monroe and his Blue Grass Boys, is one of the all-time great fiddlers. His tone, phrasing, and wealth of musical ideas will inspire anyone into old-time or bluegrass music.

The mark ◆ next to a note indicates a harmonic:

Black Mountain Rag

Weave and Way

I've known this tune for a while, but it wasn't until it appeared as a guitar-dobro duet on Norman Blake's *Home in Sulphur Springs* (Rounder 0012) that I learned its name. Norman's notes say that it's "probably an old Scotch tune."

Harmony - 2nd guitar

Weave and Way

Harmony

Devil's Dream

The Reverend Gary Davis played a finger-style *Devil's Dream* which has little relation to the tune usually known by that name. While learning the piece I asked Brother Davis what he felt the devil was dreaming about. According to the Reverend, the devil was taking a mid-day snooze, contentedly snoring away as he dreamed of tempting some fellow to sin and enter his dominion.

The variation on the B section features some involved cross-picking, during which these chord positions will be used for A6, E7, E9, and A:

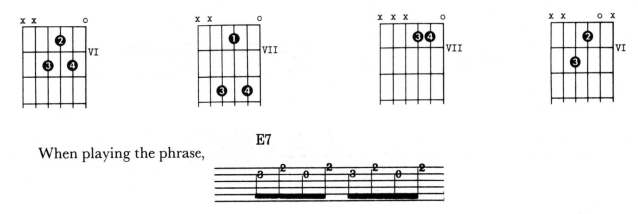

When playing the phrase,

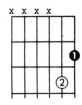

keep your first finger on F♯ and use your second finger for D:

A Bm is often substituted for the E7, creating this
chord pattern for both the A and B sections:

A / A / Bm / Bm / A / A / Bm / E⁷ A:‖

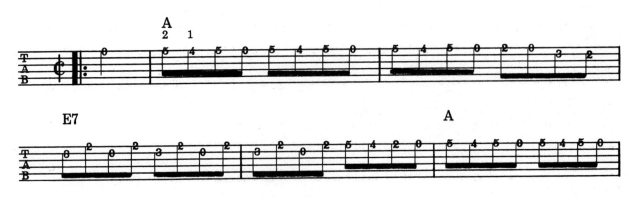

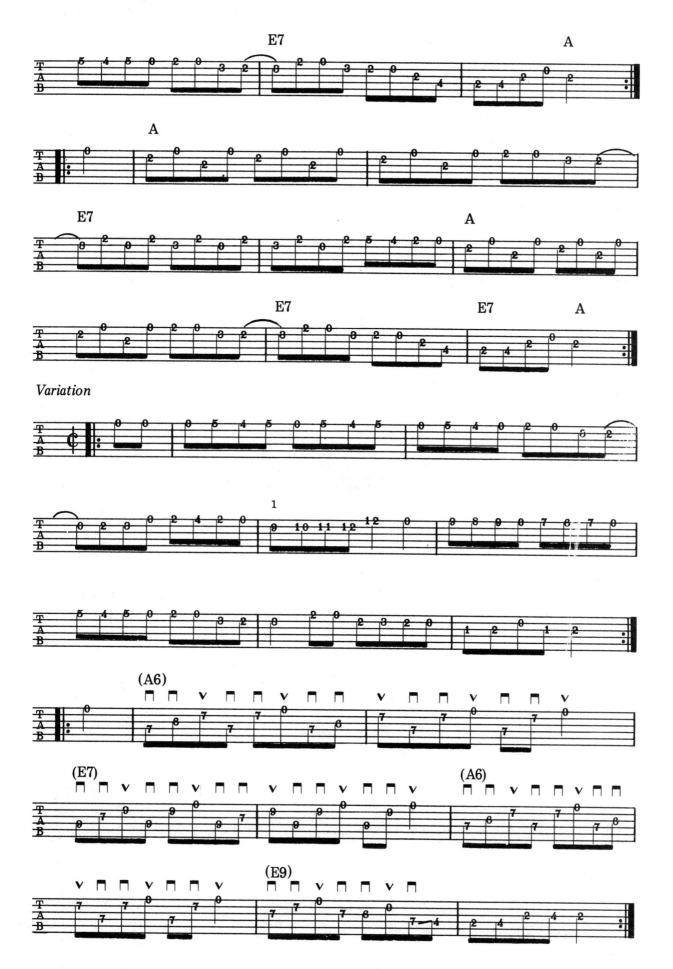

Devil's Dream

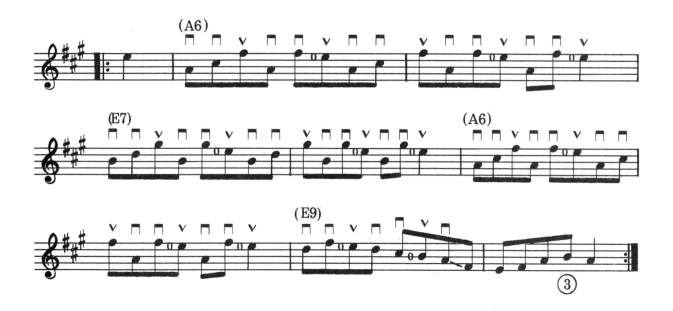

Billy in The Lowground

One or two licks from Texas fiddler Benny Thomasson's rendition (County 703) have crept into my arrangement. Clarence White flatpicks a solid *Billy in The Lowground* on *The Kentucky Colonels: Appalachian Swing* (World Pacific 1821).

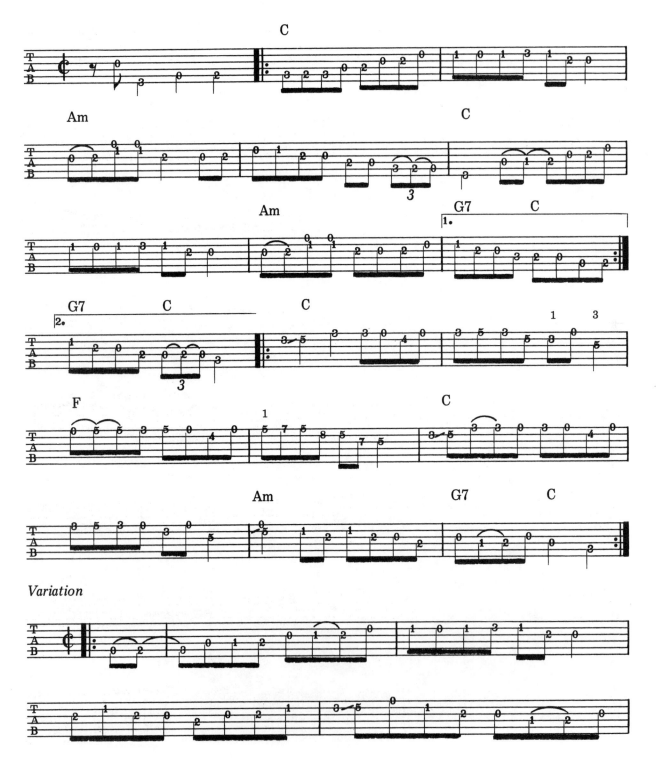

Variation

Variation

Old Joe Clark

I think I had some of the classic twin fiddle instrumentals by Bill Monroe's band in the back of my mind when I worked out this arrangement of *Old Joe Clark*.

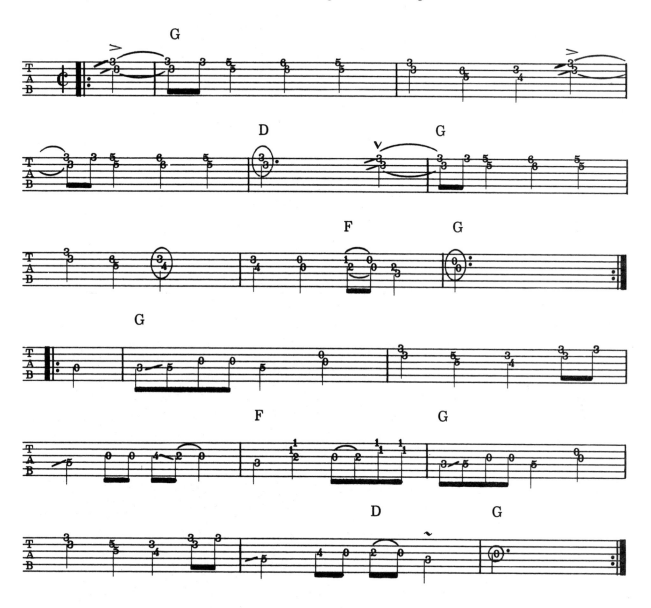

Old Joe Clark

Paddy on the Turnpike

Paddy on the Turnpike is a striking and beautiful Irish reel. The bluegrassers have changed it a great deal and often play it in the major rather than the minor key; this arrangement is closer to the older way of playing it.

One of the peculiar qualities of the piece is the alternation between the F♮ and F♯. This necessitates using a D7 rather than an F chord for the first half of the third measure. A Dm7 may be substituted for the F chord throughout the piece.

Kenny Baker's *First Day in Town* was inspired by this tune and also works out well on the guitar. First Day in Town can be found on Kenny's first solo recording, *Portrait of a Bluegrass Fiddler* (County 719).

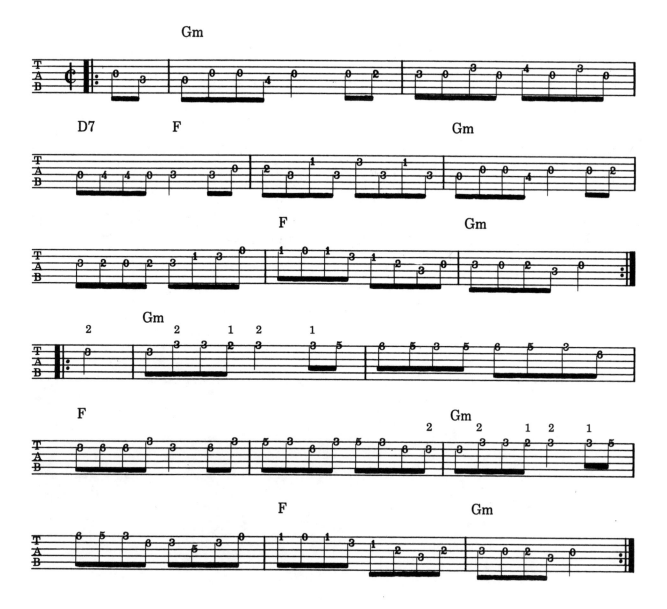

Paddy on the Turnpike

The Eighth of January

The Eighth of January commemorates the Battle of New Orleans. Jimmie Driftwood wrote lyrics to it a while back and the tune became a pop hit.

In the opening phrase of the variation, pick the pickup note (F) and bend it up to F♯ on the first beat of the next measure, using only one attack.

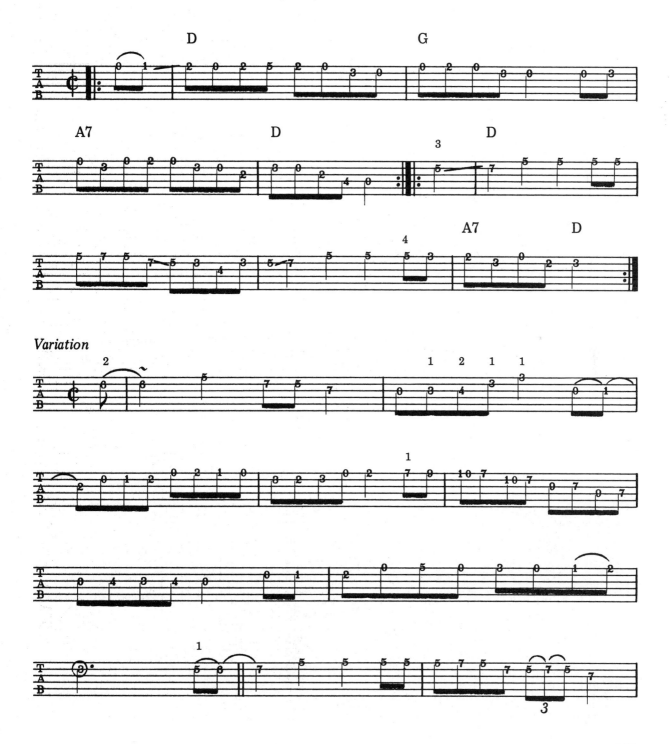

Variation

Sail Away Ladies

Uncle Dave Macon recorded a song based on this old-time tune. My arrangement was largely inspired by Kenny Baker's great rendition of the tune on *A Baker's Dozen* (County 730). Kenny has his back-up boys throw some minor chords in, which gives the tune a somewhat mellower feel. Try the tune out with these chords after playing the standard three chord version:

‖G / Em / C / G / G / Am / D7 / G:‖

‖G / Am / D7 / G / G / Am / D7 / G:‖

105

Flop-Eared Mule

When playing the pickup arpeggios on the G and D chords use a single downstroke, letting the pick quickly glide over the 4th, 3rd, 2nd and 1st strings.

Instead of sounding the open G on contact, mute the unfretted 3rd string with the second or third finger of your left hand, so that the pick produces a percussive effect. The muted string is indicated by an "x" in the notation.

The descending D7 lick,

is based around these positions:

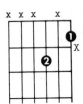 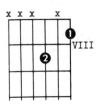 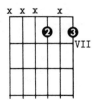 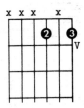

When playing the 1st and 3rd strings together, mute the unfretted 2nd string with your left hand and use a single downstroke to sound both notes simultaneously.

108

The Humors of Lisadel

I first heard this beautiful lilting Irish reel from my friend Tom Gallagher, who picked it up over in Ireland. The Irish-style embellishments (triplets, slurs, etc.) present a challenge to the guitarist.

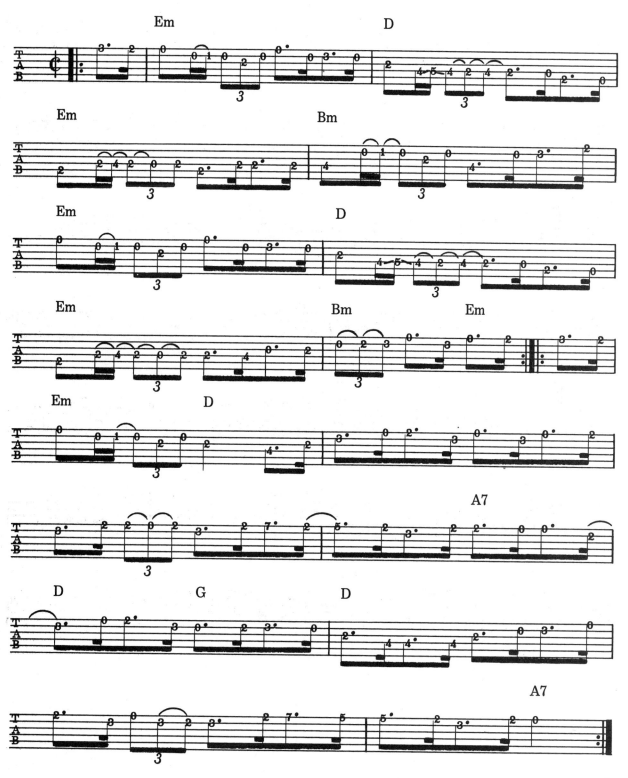

The Humors of Lisadel

Salt River

Doc Watson flatpicks a mean *Salt River* on *Doc Watson on Stage* (VSD 9/10). Fiddler Lewis Franklin comes up with some exciting variations on the melody in his performance of the tune on *Texas Fiddle Favorites* (County 707). Listening to good Texas fiddlers will provide you with plenty of melodic ideas to fool around with when you improvise.

Salt River

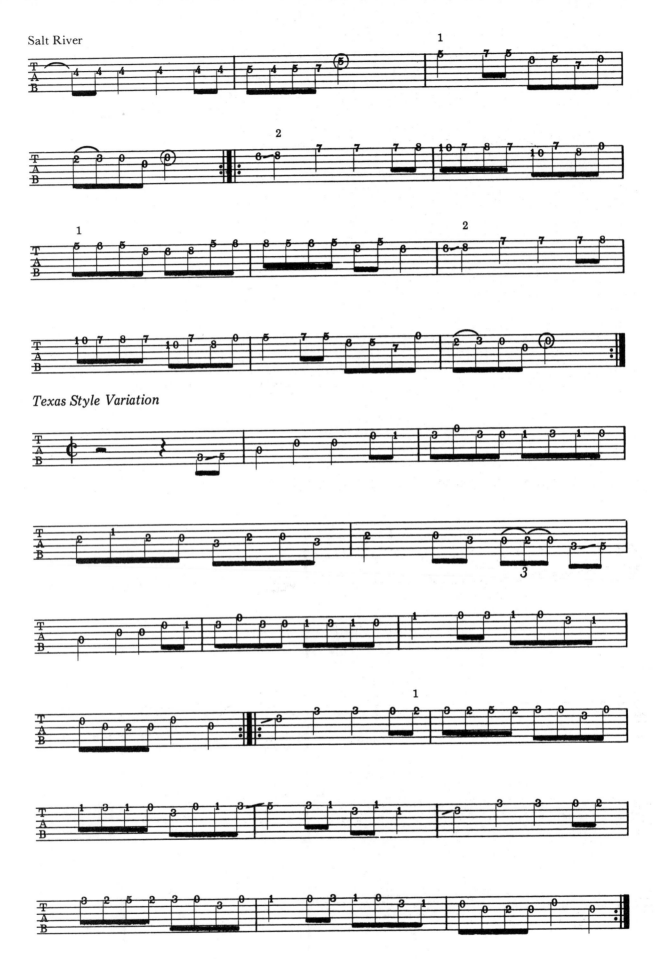

Texas Style Variation

Harmony

Salt River

Stoney Creek
by Jim and Jesse McReynolds

Jim and Jesse and the Virginia Boys' classic recording of this bluegrass instrumental can be found on *Bluegrass Special* (Epic BN 26031).

The first two measures of the bridge employ cross-picking.

Begin with an F position,

and shift to this position, in the following measure.

An E9, is found at the end of the bridge.

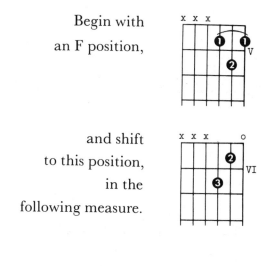

The rhythm guitar comes to a stop for a measure when the phrase appears:

The rhythm man can play a figure like

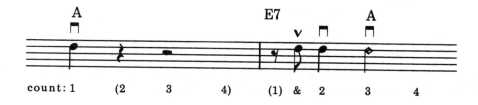

Stoney Creek

Stoney Creek

Cotton Patch Rag

Cotton Patch Rag is popular with Texas fiddlers. Lewis Franklin gives the tune a real work-out on County 707.

In the cross-picking section hold a partial C, for the C part

and an F triad, for the F part.

Intros and Tags

This is the most common way of kicking off a tune:

It can also be played with double stops:

Another way to begin a number is to allow the lead instrument to take the first bar alone, and to have the rhythm instrument enter during the second bar.

Here are a few "tag" endings you can slap on to the end of a tune. You should have no trouble constructing your own.

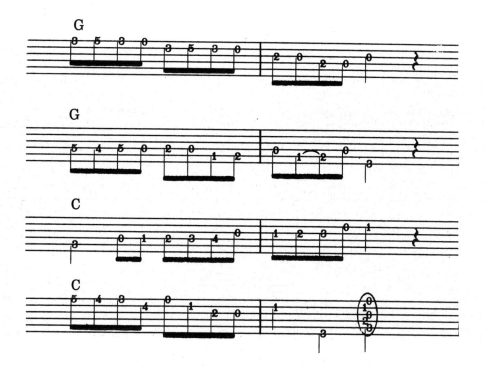

Playing Back-up

Any fiddler or lead man appreciates a solid rhythm guitar behind him. The quality of the back-up guitar work affects the overall sound of the music being played. A good rhythm player supports the fiddler and helps establish a strong danceable rhythm; a mediocre back-up makes for a disjointed performance and can throw even a good fiddler off the track.

The basic type of back-up used behind fiddle tunes is a 4/4 bass-strum, bass-strum rhythm:

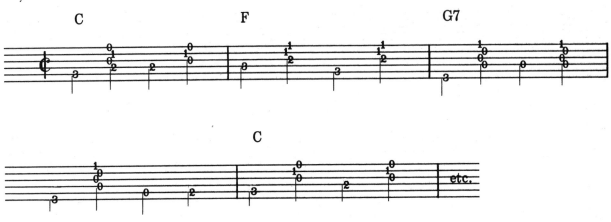

At times you may desire to fill the rhythm out more:

The bass-strum rhythm is sometimes interrupted by single note runs:

The ability to use bass runs tastefully and in a manner that propels the rhythm is one of the trademarks of a good old-time or bluegrass back-up guitar player. A guitarist who gets carried away with his runs often loses the rhythm and defeats his purpose of supporting the lead instrument. The back-up should always compliment rather than compete with the lead.

Here are typical rhythm parts for *Ragtime Annie, Cripple Creek* and *Sailor's Hornpipe.* Notice that in *Cripple Creek* the second beat of the bar sometimes receives an accent.

Sailor's Hornpipe

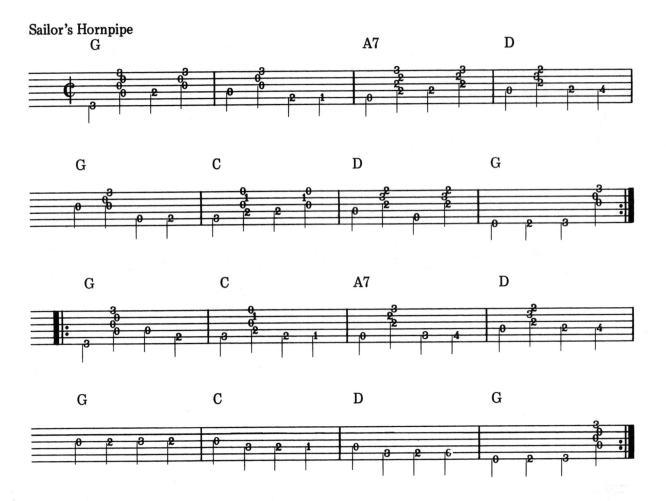

Texas fiddlers play their tunes more slowly and with more of a "swing" rhythm than do Southeasterners; consequently, the style of back-up differs. In Texas-style fiddle music, a piano and tenor guitar often join the standard guitar as rhythm instruments. The guitarist plays what is called a "sock" rhythm using barred chords in addition to open ones, and only occasionally connects his chords with runs.

Try out a "sock" rhythm back-up for "Fisher's Hornpipe" using these chords: D, G, B7, E7, A7, G♯ dim.

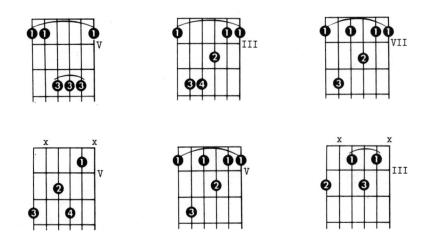

To play the "sock" rhythm, play four strums to the bar, on the beat, cutting the second and fourth beats short by releasing your left hand pressure. On the G7 and G♯ diminished chords be sure to mute those strings marked "x" in the diagrams, so that only the fretted strings sound.

Here is a chord-progression for a Texas-style back up for "Fisher's Hornpipe." Notice that a "circle of fifths" progression (B7-E7-A7-D) has been introduced.

Fisher's Hornpipe

Suggested Listening

County 507—*Old Time Fiddle Classics*
County 527—*Old Time Fiddle Classics—Vol. 2*
County 719—Kenny Baker: *Portrait of a Bluegrass Fiddler*
County 730—Kenny Baker: *Baker's Dozen*
County 714—Kenny Baker and Joe Greene: *High Country*
County 722—*Joe Greene's Fiddle Album*
County 725—The Riendeau Family: *Old Time Fiddling From New England*
County 703—Bartow Riley, Benny Thomasson, Vernon Solomon: *Texas Hoedown*
County 707—Lewis Franklin, Major Franklin, Norman Solomon: *Texas Fiddle Favorites*
County 724—Benny Thomasson: *Country Fiddling From The Big State*
County 701—Kyle Creed, Wade Ward, Fred Cockerham: *Clawhammer Banjo*
County 713—Tommy Jarrel, Fred Cockerham, Oscar Jenkins: *Down at Cider Mill*
County 723—Jenkins, Jarrel, and Cockerham: *Back Home in the Blue Ridge*
Vanguard VSD 79152—*Doc Watson*
Vanguard VSD 79170—*Doc Watson and Son*
Vanguard VSD 79276—*Doc Watson in Nashville*
Vanguard VSD 6566—Doc Watson: *Ballads From Deep Gap*
Vanguard VSD 9/10—*Doc Watson on Stage*
American Heritage AHLP 275—Dan Crary: *Bluegrass Guitar*
World Pacific 1821—Kentucky Colonels: *Appalachian Swing with Clarence and Roland White*
Rural Rhythm RRBR 244—*Fiddling Buck Ryan with Reno and Smiley* (Reno turns in some fine guitar work here).
King 701—Reno and Smiley: *Country Songs* (Great singing, tasty guitar by Reno).
Decca DL 14601—Bill Monroe and his Blue Grass Boys: *Bluegrass Instrumentals*
Epic BN 26031—Jim and Jesse and the Virginia Boys: *Bluegrass Special*
UAS 9801—Nitti Gritti Dirt Band with Maybelle Carter, Doc Watson, Merle Travis, Jimmy Martin, Vassar Clements, Earl Scruggs, Roy Acuff and others: *Will The Circle Be Unbroken* (Plenty of fine music here and good country guitar in a variety of styles).

Most of these records are available by mail from County Sales, 307 E. 37 St., New York, N.Y. 10016.

Bibliography

O'Neill's Music of Ireland (available from Dan Collins, 1375 Crosby Ave., Bronx, New York 10461).
Cole's One Thousand Fiddle Tunes (M.M. Cole Publishing Co., 251 Grand Ave., Chicago, Ill. 60611)